viola

essential Musicianship for strings

FUNDAMENTAL ensemble concepts

Michael Allen
Robert Gillespie
Pamela Tellejohn Hayes

Table of Contents

Unit	Page
D Major Rounds	2
D Major Arrangements	3
G Major Rounds	6
G Major Arrangements Lower Octave (Violin)	7
C Major Rounds	10
C Major Arrangements	11
G Major Rounds	14
G Major Arrangements Upper Octave (Violin)	15

ISBN 1-4234-3102-2

Copyright © 2006 by HAL LEONARD CORPORATION
International Copyright Secured   All Rights Reserved

7777 W. BLUEMOUND RD. P.O. BOX 13819 MILWAUKEE, WI 53213

D Major Rounds

D Major Arrangements

London Bridge
English Folk Song

Michael Row The Boat Ashore
American Folk Song

Musette
Johann Sebastian Bach

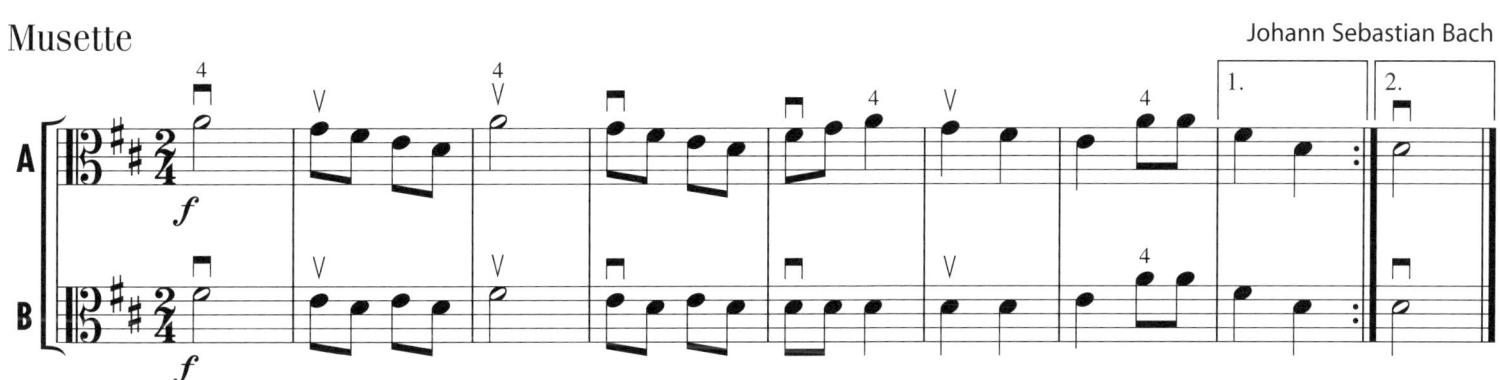

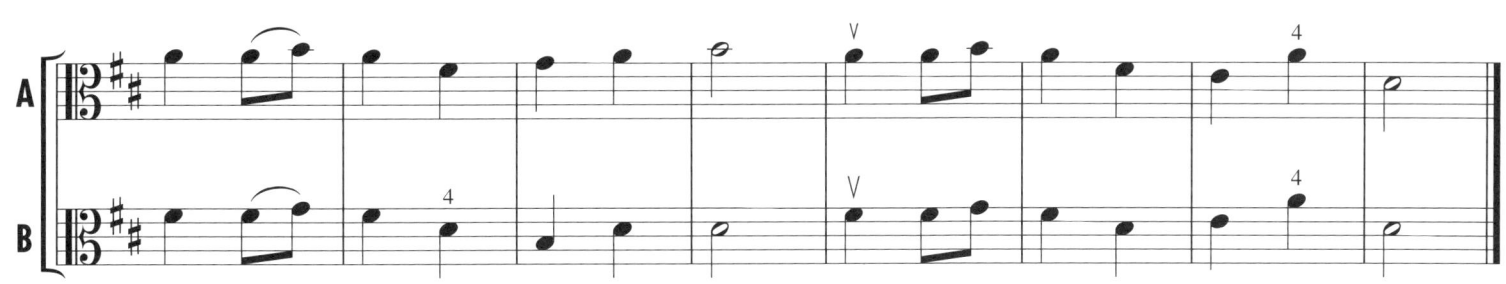

Toe Tapping
Michael Allen

Round Dance
German Barndance

G Major Lower Octave (Violin) Arrangements

This Old Man
American Folk Song

Buffalo Gals
American Cowboy Song

Lullaby

Johannes Brahms

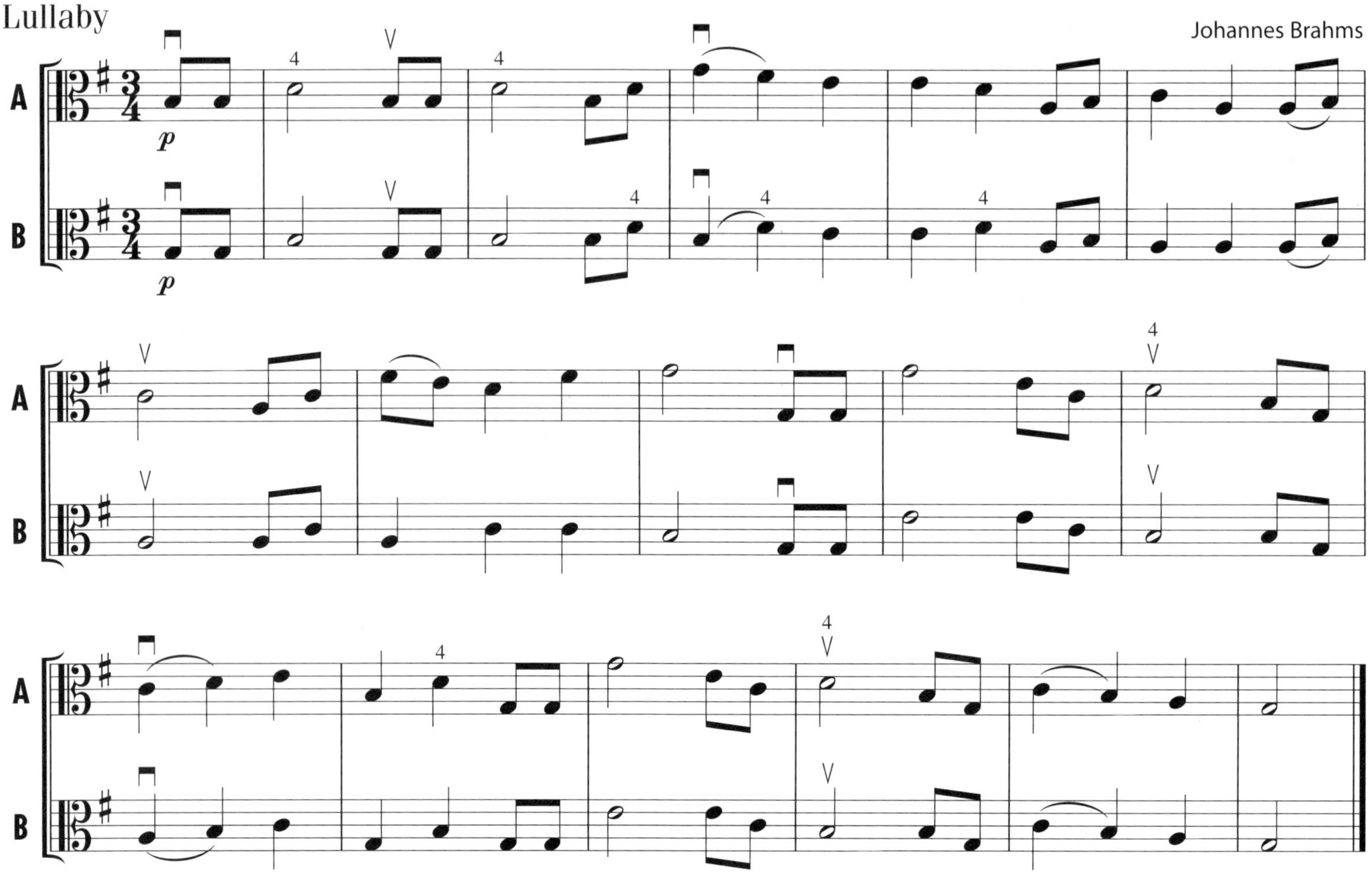

French Folk Song

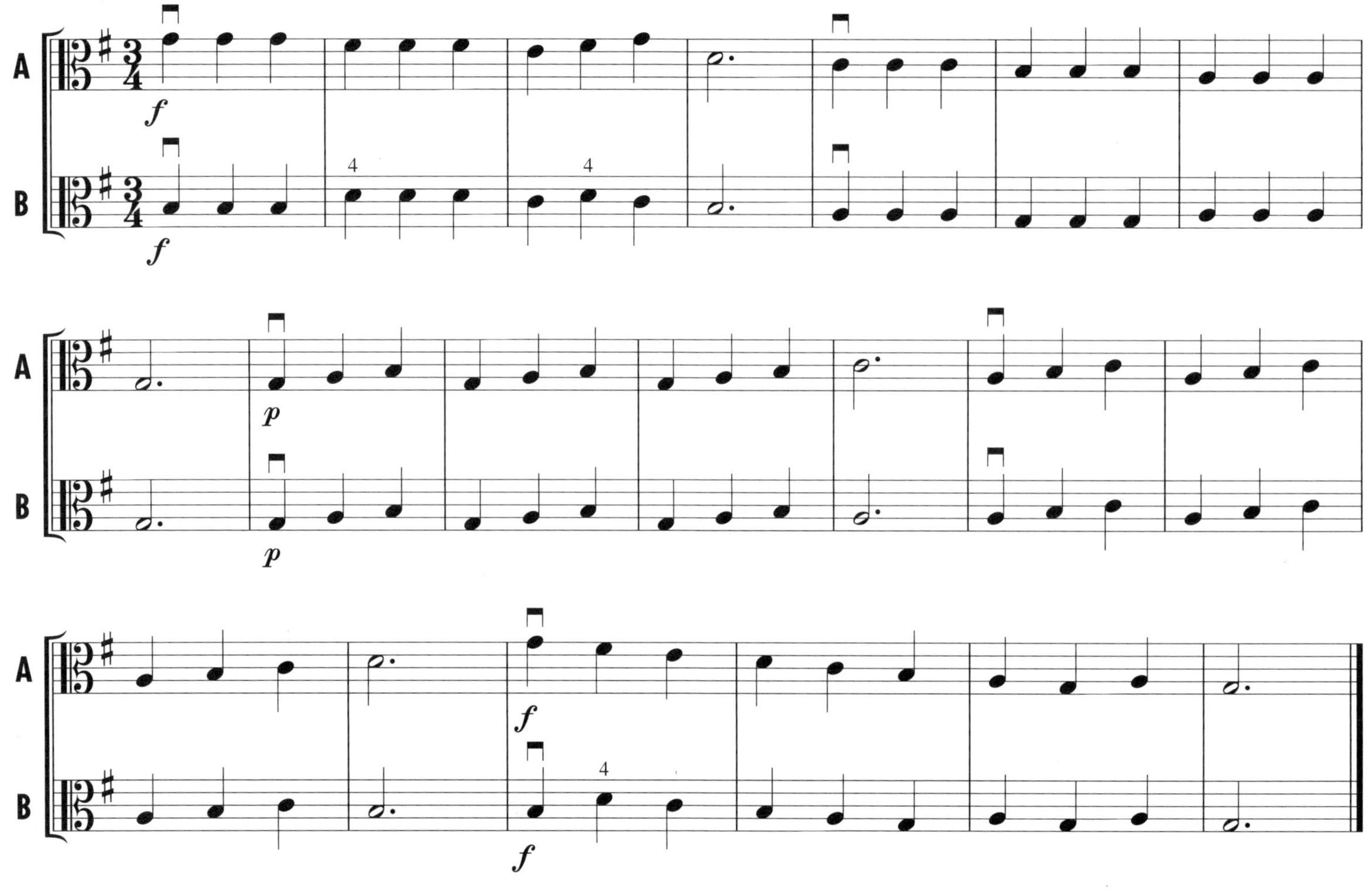

String Concepts – Fundamental Level

Jingli Nona — Far Eastern Folk Song

Friday Night Polka — Michael Allen

C Major Rounds

C Major Arrangements

Long, Long Ago
T. H. Bayly

Monday's Melody
Traditional Folk Song

Chanukah
Israeli Folk Song

Blue Bells Of Scotland
Scottish Folk Song

The Orchestra Song – 5 Parts

Old Quodlibet

String Concepts – Fundamental Level

G Major Rounds

Flying Around
English

Sailing on the Avon
English

Haste
Samuel Arnold

White Coral Bells
Great Britain

G Major Upper Octave (Violin) Arrangements

Minuet — Johann Sebastian Bach

Cielito Lindo — Mexican Folk Song

The Jolly Boatman
English Folk Song

Botany Bay
Australian Folk Song